Benno Loewy, James Orchard Halliwell-Phillipps

A List of Works Illustrative of the Life and Writings of Shakespeare

The History of Stratford-on-Avon and the Rise and Progress of the Early

English Drama

Benno Loewy, James Orchard Halliwell-Phillipps

A List of Works Illustrative of the Life and Writings of Shakespeare
The History of Stratford-on-Avon and the Rise and Progress of the Early English ·
Drama

ISBN/EAN: 9783337412524

Printed in Europe, USA, Canada, Australia, Japan

Cover: Foto ©Thomas Meinert / pixelio.de

More available books at **www.hansebooks.com**

A LIST OF WORKS

ILLUSTRATIVE OF THE LIFE AND WRITINGS OF

SHAKESPEARE,

THE HISTORY OF STRATFORD-ON-AVON, AND

THE RISE AND PROGRESS OF THE

EARLY ENGLISH DRAMA,

PRINTED FOR VERY LIMITED AND PRIVATE

CIRCULATION AT THE EXPENSE

OF J. O. HALLIWELL.

1850-1866.

LONDON:

1867.

PREFACE.

HE object sought to be accomplished by the some-
what peculiar mode of circulation herein adopted,
is the preservation of a vast quantity of Shakespearian materials, useful to the student and critical reader,
which are either too diffuse or too technical to be included in
works prepared for the general public.

Some of that numerous class, who believe they can always
regulate the affairs of their neighbours to advantage, have very
strongly advised me to increase the numbers of the impression of
these books, and to lower their price. The argument, on the
first statement, appears conclusive. It is this:—when once
the type is set, the printing of five hundred copies costs little
more than ten. Instead, therefore, in the case, for instance,
of a book, the expenses for ten copies of which amount to £20,
issuing ten copies at £2 each, I were to print five hundred at
the moderate price of five shillings each, in the place of merely
clearing the expenses I should (allowing for the extra cost of

paper and binding) not only realize a profit of about £70 on a single small book, but please a larger number of people, do far greater good to literature, &c, &c.

Now, although I can afford to work at these favourite studies without the prospect of remuneration, I am not sufficiently well off—who is, in these mercenary days?—to despise by any means the pleasing contemplation of substantial profits. The scheme, however, is not practicable, for this simple reason. The numbers of copies, small as they are, are the *utmost* that I can attend to *personally.* The collation, transmission, and keeping the accounts, entail, as it is, a sufficient encroachment on my time ; the continual exhaustion of the impressions of some of the books merely leaving places vacant for new ones. If I were to print and retain large stocks of these works, I should have to take a house on purpose for the business, to keep clerks, with dozens of ledgers, and, even then, I am pretty well convinced that the notion of profits would be visionary. It looks remarkably well on paper, but five hundred copies of this class of books would not be disposed of for many years, and the expenses and loss of interest on the original outlay would either swallow up the margin of supposed profit, or reduce it to an insignificant amount. Even in the case of the works named in the following list, there is, at the lowest calculation, a sum of three thousand pounds sank beyond the subscriptions actually received up to the present time. It is true that, in the long run, I expect to recover all of this from the large increase of value anticipated in those cases where small stocks remain ; but business people, who understand the uses of money, know that, under these circumstances, there should be a considerable overplus of receipts merely to meet interest, if " both ends" are to " meet."

I have entered into these particulars, in reply to several urgent applications to me to render these works more accessible. The decision turns on what is practicable, not on what we should exactly like ; and those who inveigh so bitterly against the system of small limits should bear in mind that the surest method of obtaining subscribers to expensive works is the knowledge of the probability that, if they do not subscribe at once, they either miss them altogether, or obtain them afterwards only at an extravagant rate. With what I believe to be important Shakespearian objects in view, I have adopted, to attain those objects, the *only* plan which I sincerely believe to be practicable in the hands of any one, at least, who is not a millionaire.

J. O. HALLIWELL.

No. 6, St. Mary's Place, West Brompton,
near London, January, 1867.

THE FOLIO SHAKESPEARE.

HE WORKS OF WILLIAM SHAKE-
SPEARE, the Text formed from a new collation
of the early Editions ; to which are added all the
original Novels and Tales on which the Plays are founded ;
copious archæological Annotations on each Play ; an Essay on
the Formation of the Text; and a Life of the Poet. By
J. O. Halliwell, Esq. F.R.S.

The wood-engravings and copper-plates by the late F. W.
Fairholt, Esq. F.S.A. The lithographic facsimiles by E. W.
Ashbee, Esq.

Sixteen Volumes, folio, 1853–1865.

The impression limited to one hundred and fifty copies, in
twenty-five of which the plates are on India paper.

Subscription—Plain paper, new . . £105.

      ,,   ditto,   second-hand, £75.

      ,,   India paper, new . . £150.

      ,,   ditto,   second hand, £100.

The blocks and plates of the numerous woodcuts, facsimiles,
and engravings, used in this work, have been destroyed.

*** The possession of second-hand copies arises from my having purchased, during the fourteen years which have now elapsed since the work was commenced, several copies from original subscribers, and from the executors of deceased subscribers.

Some of the copies have changed hands three or four times, and alterations of proprietorship may of course have occurred without my knowledge. In every copy the first nine volumes are attested with the number assigned to that copy, and the following is an accurate list of owners of the work on this day (January 4th, 1867) so far as I know them, arranged according to the order in which the copies are numbered, the numbers left blank belonging to the copies now in my possession : —

1. The Public Library, Plymouth.

2. The Newark Stock Library.

3. The Hon. Society of Lincoln's Inn.

4. London Institution.

5. The University of St. Andrews.

6. W. H. Riggs, Esq. New York.

7. Captain Charles Gibbs.

8. B. G. Windus, Esq.

9. Charles Walton, Esq.

10. James Parker, Esq.

11. The Duke of Devonshire, K.G.

12. Dr. Bell Fletcher.

13. D. D. Hopkyns, Esq.

14. Miss Mather.

15. A. W. Griswold, Esq. New York.

16. Mrs. Bailey, Easton Court.

17. Messrs. Willis & Sotheran.

18. Thomas Turpin, Esq. now in U. S.

19. John Weston, Esq.

20. Lieut.-Col. Macdonald Macdonald.

21. Robert Lang, Esq.

22. J. G. Woodhouse, Esq.

23.

24. S. A. Philbrick, Esq.

25. J. B. Davis, Esq. M.D.

26. Thomas B. Parsons, Esq.

27. Alexander Farnum, Esq. U. S.

28. Henry William Peek, Esq.

29. The Rev. Archibald Weir.

30. E. T. Carson, Esq. Cincinnati.

31. The Earl of Warwick.

32. William P. Hunt, Esq.

33. The Duke of Buccleuch and Queensberry, K.G.

34. R. S. Holford, Esq. M.P.

35. W. F. Fowle, Esq. Boston, U. S.

36. John Durdin, Esq.

37. Travers B. Wire, Esq.

38. Alfred George, Esq.

39. John Staunton, Esq.

40. The Peabody Institute, Baltimore.

41. Henry Hucks Gibbs, Esq.

42. Plowden C. J. Weston, Esq.

43. Mortimer Harris, Esq.

44. William Euing, Esq.

45. Frederick Ouvry, Esq. Treas. S. A.

46. Lord Londesborough.

47. Lord Houghton.

48. The Hon. E. C. Curzon.

49. John Fitchett Marsh, Esq.

50. The Duke of Newcastle.

51. H. T. D. Bathurst, Esq.

52. Sebastian Bazley, Esq.

53.

54. Mr. Quaritch.

India Paper — 55. Robert McConnell, Esq. *now W. Kelly*

56.

57. William Atkinson, Esq. Ashton Hayes.

58. William J. Clement, Esq. M.P.

59. G. G. Mounsey, Esq.

60. William Harrison, Esq. F.S.A.

61. Sterling Westhorp, Esq.

62. James Mackenzie, Esq. Edinburgh.

63. The Rev. William Borlase.

64.. William Horsfall, Esq.

65. Thomas Coombs, Esq.

66. Noel Paton, Esq. Edinburgh.

67.. The British Museum.

68. Harman Grisewood, Esq.

69. George Livermore, Esq. Boston, U. S.

70. John Bailey Langborne, Esq.

71. The City Library, Guildhall.

72. Hull Subscription Library.

73. The Royal Dublin Society.

74. The Liverpool Free Library.

75. William H. Crawford, Esq.

76. Charles Winn, Esq. Nostell Priory.

77. James Pilkington, Esq.

78. William B. Astor, Esq. New York.
79. The Astor Library.

80. Henry Allsopp, Esq.

81. William Henry Brown, Esq.

82. John B. Jell, Esq.

83. Sir William Jardine, Bart.

84. Lord Farnham, K.P.

85. The Royal Library, Berlin.

86. Samuel Timmins, Esq.

87. Stirling's Public Library, Glasgow.

88. William Leaf, Esq. Streatham.

89. His Excellency M. Van de Weyer.

90. Edwin Forrest, Esq. Philadelphia.

91. William Tyssen Amhurst, Esq.

92. Sir Harford J. J. Brydges, Bart.

93. The University Library, Cambridge.

94. A. Smollett, Esq. Levenfield.

95. John C. Nicholl, Esq.

96. The Society of Antiquaries.

97. The Bodleian Library.

98.

99. Robert P. Rayne, Esq. New Orleans.

100. Dr. Buchanan Washbourn.

101.

102.

103. The Athenæum Club.

104. S. A. R. le Duc d'Aumale.

105.

106. Sir John Bethune, Bart.

107. T. S. Godfrey, Esq.

108. George Washington Riggs, Esq. U. S.

109. E. L. S. Benzon, Esq.

110. Thomas P. Barton, Esq. New York.

111. Robert Lenox Kennedy, Esq. New York.

112. The University Library, Glasgow.

113. John Haes, Esq.

114. The House of Commons.

115. Baron Rothschild.

116.

117. St. John's College, Cambridge.

118. Messrs. Asher & Co. Berlin.

119.

120. Professor Hoegel, Vienna.

121. Charles Leaf, Esq.

122. Viscount Falmouth.

123. The Imperial Court of Austria.

124. George W. Whistler, Esq.

125. James Lenox, Esq. New York.

126 to 128. Three Copies sent to the United States, through Mr. Sidney S. Rider, of Providence.

129. Mr. Allen, for the U. S.

130.

131.

132.

133.

134.

135.

136.

137.

138.

139.

140.

141.

142.

143.

144.

145.

146.

147. Henry Huth, Esq.

148.

149.

150. The Editor's own copy.

A list of the countries through which the 122 copies absolutely disposed of are distributed may be worth adding :—

England	78 copies.
Scotland	11 copies.
Wales	2 copies.
Ireland	3 copies.
The United States . .	22 copies.
Prussia	2 copies.
Austria	2 copies.
France	1 copy.
Belgium	1 copy.
	122 copies.
In the Editor's possession .	28 copies.
Total . .	150 copies.

MISCELLANIES.

MISCELLANIES.

A NEW Boke about Shakespeare and Stratford-on-Avon. Quarto, 1850. *Out of Print.*

2. Shakespeare's Will, printed with the original Interlineations, with a few Preliminary Observations. Quarto, 1851. *Out of Print.*

3. Some Account of Antiquities, Coins, Manuscripts, Rare Books, Ancient Documents, and other Reliques, illustrative of the Life and Works of Shakespeare. Quarto, 1852. *Out of Print.*

4. Observations on the Shakespearian Documents at Bridgewater House, with a facsimile of the Southampton Letter. Quarto, 1853. *Out of Print.*

5. A Garland of Shakespeariana. Quarto, 1854. *Out of Print.*

6. A Lyttle Boke gevinge a True and Briefe Accounte of Shakespearian Reliques and Curiosities. Quarto, 1856. *Out of Print.*

7. A Brief Hand-List of Books, Manuscripts, &c, illustrative of the Life and Writings of Shakespeare, collected between the years 1842 and 1859. Octavo, 1859. *Out of Print.*

8. Shaksperian Drolls, from a rare Book printed in the year 1698, containing the Mad Wooing, and the Boaster, or Bully Huff catch'd in a Trap. Square 12mo. 1859. *Out of Print.*

9. Fortune's Tennis Ball, an old Poem on the same Story which Shakespeare used in the Winter's Tale. Quarto, 1859. *Out of Print.*

10. A Brief Hand-List of the early Quarto Editions of the Plays of Shakespeare, with Notices of the old Impressions of the Poems. Octavo, 1860. *Out of Print.*

11. The Merry Conceited Humours of Bottom the Weaver, a Droll Compound out of the Comic Scenes of the Midsummer Night's Dream in 1646. Square 12mo. 1860. *Out of Print.*

12. A Skeleton Hand-List of the early Quarto Editions of the Plays of Shakespeare. Octavo, 1860. *Out of Print.*

13. The Ancient Ballad of the Fair Widow of Watling Street and her Three Daughters, from the earliest known Edition printed by Thomas Pavier about the year 1600. Square 12mo. 1860. *Out of Print.*

14. Facsimile Copies taken from the Edition of Shakespeare's Tragedy of Hamlet dated in 1605, made for the purpose of showing that it is the same impression as that of 1604, the date only being altered. Quarto, 1860. *Out of Print.*

15. The Droll of the Bouncing Knight, taken from the Play of Henry the Fourth, and acted about the year 1642. Square 12mo. 1860. *Out of Print.*

16. Facsimiles of the Plats of Old English Plays, being the original Directions for the Actors suspended near the Prompters' Station on the Walls of the Fortune Theatre. Folio, 1860. *Out of Print.*

17. The Debate and Stryfe betwene Somer and Wynter; a poetical Dialogue supposed to have furnished a hint for Love's Labour's Lost. Square 12mo. 1860. *Out of Print.*

18. A Hand-List of upwards of a Thousand Volumes of Shakespeariana. Small quarto, 1862. *Out of Print.*

19. A Brief Hand-List of the Records belonging to the Borough of Stratford-on-Avon, with Notes of a Few of the Shakesperian Documents in the same Collection. Small quarto, 1862. *Out of Print.*

20. A Brief Hand-List of the Collections respecting the Life and Works of Shakespeare, and the History and Antiquities of Stratford-upon-Avon, formed by the late R. B. Wheler. Small quarto, 1863. *Out of Print.*

21. Shakespearian Facsimiles; a Collection of Curious and Interesting Documents, Plans, Signatures, &c, illustrative of the Biography of Shakespeare and the History of his Family; from the Originals chiefly Preserved at Stratford-on-Avon. The Facsimiles by E. W. Ashbee, Esq. Folio, 1863. *Out of Print.*

22. A Descriptive Calendar of the Ancient Manuscripts and Records in the Possession of the Corporation of Stratford-upon-Avon ; including Notices of Shakespeare and his Family, and of several Persons connected with the Poet. Folio, 1863. A thick volume, uniform with the Folio Shakespeare. Seventy-five Copies printed. Subscription, £4. 4s.

23. An Historical Account of the New Place, Stratford-upon-Avon, the Last Residence of Shakespeare. With numerous Engravings. Folio, 1864. *For Presents only.*

24. Stratford-upon-Avon in the Times of the Shakespeares, illustrated by Extracts from the Council Books of the Corporation, selected especially with Reference to the History of the Poet's Father. Illustrated with Facsimiles of the Entries respecting John Shakespeare, executed by E. W. Ashbee, Esq. Folio, 1864. *Out of Print.*

25. A Hand-Book Index to the Works of Shakespeare, including References to the Phrases, Manners, Customs, Proverbs, Songs, Particles, &c, which are used or alluded to by the Great Dramatist. Octavo, 1866. Pp. 551. Fifty Copies printed. Subscription, £3. 3s.

BOOKS

ILLUSTRATIVE OF THE LIFE AND WORKS

OF SHAKESPEARE,

THE HISTORY OF STRATFORD - ON - AVON, AND

THE ANNALS OF THE OLD

ENGLISH STAGE,

IN SQUARE DUODECIMO, SMALL OCTAVO, AND SMALL QUARTO.

THE IMPRESSION LIMITED TO TEN COPIES.

BOOKS OF TEN COPIES.

IT has long been my wish to see preserved the more valuable of the transcripts and collections made in illustration of the above subjects during the last quarter of a century, otherwise I may, like Malone, die, leaving the results of much laborious research to be scattered and lost. It is scarcely necessary to observe that there are numerous papers, important for the student to consult in a complete state, which could not be introduced in extenso into any Life or Commentary on Shakespeare, of however comprehensive a character.

In addition to the collections I already have, I should wish to include the very curious documents, hitherto unknown, illustrative of the early English stage, which I have lately discovered at Ipswich, Ludlow, &c, and in the Public Record Office, and an experienced record-reader must be employed to ransack all such sources. In short, I shall spare no expense to complete this important series of material.

The limitation to Ten Copies may seem very exclusive, but

it must be recollected that I shall have to collate, register, and certify *every copy*, and my time is so much occupied I could hardly undertake this were the number more extensive.

Each book will form a separate volume, not marked as belonging to a series, and of various sizes to suit various documents and illustrations. Many will be of the quaint sizes issued from the Whittingham Press. The subscriptions will of course be of varied amount, but the cost of no single volume will exceed two guineas.

Complete sets are now impossible to be obtained, but the numbers marked with an asterisk are at present to be subscribed for either separately or collectively; and each volume is quite distinct and complete by itself.

1. The Correspondence of Edmond Malone, the Editor of Shakespeare, with the Rev. James Davenport, D.D., Vicar of Stratford-on-Avon. Quarto, 1864. *Out of Print.*

2. Beware the Cat, 1570, an exceedingly rare and curious Rhapsody, containing matters illustrative of the History of the Stage. Small quarto, 1864. *Out of Print.*

3. Extracts from ancient Subsidy Rolls, showing the Values of goods and Lands upon which Assessments were made in respect to the Inhabitants of Stratford-upon-Avon. Small quarto, 1864. *Out of Print.*

4. Original Collections on Shakespeare and Stratford-on-Avon, by John Jordan, the Stratford Poet; selected from the Original Manuscripts written about the year 1780. Quarto, 1864. *Out of Print.*

5. A Hand-Table of Regnal Years for the Use of Inquirers into the History of the Shakespeares. Octavo, 1864. *Out of Print.*

6. Contemporary Depositions respecting an affray at Norwich in the year 1583, in which Queen Elizabeth's Company of Players, then acting at the Red Lion Inn, were involved. Square 12mo. 1864. *Out of Print.*

7. Original Letters from Edmond Malone, the Editor of Shakespeare, to John Jordan, the Poet, now first printed from the autograph Manuscripts preserved at Stratford-on-Avon. Quarto, 1864. *Out of Print.*

8. Extracts of Entries respecting Shakespeare, his Family and Connections, carefully taken from the original Parish Registers preserved in the Church of the Holy Trinity at Stratford-on-Avon. Quarto, 1864. *Out of Print.*

9. Was Nicholas ap Roberts that Butcher's Son of Stratford-

on-Avon who is recorded by Aubrey as having been an acquaintance of Shakespeare in the early days of that great Poet? Square 12mo. 1864. *Out of Print.*

10.* Some Account of Tofte's Alba, 1598, an extremely rare Poem, containing the earliest extrinsic Notice of Shakespeare's Comedy of Love's Labour's Lost.   Square 12mo. 1865.

11. Newes from Virginia and the Island of Devils, otherwise called Bermoothawes, 1610.   Reprinted from an unique Tract. Square 12mo. 1865. *Out of Print.*

12.   A Selection from an unpublished Glossary of Provincial Words in Use in Warwickshire in the early Part of the Present Century.   Square 12mo. 1865.   *Out of Print.*

13.* The Remonstrance of Nathan Field, one of Shakespeare's Company of Actors, addressed to a Preacher in Southwark who had been arraigning against the Players at the Globe Theatre in the Year 1616.   Square 12mo. 1865.

14. The Abstract of Title to the House in Henley Street, Stratford-on-Avon, in which Shakespeare was born.   Quarto, 1865. *Out of Print.*

15. The Will of Sir Hugh Clopton, of New Place, Stratford-ou-Avon, and Citizen, Mercer, and Alderman of London, 1496. Square 12mo. 1865. *Out of Print.*

16. Those Songs and Poems from the excessively rare first Edition of England's Helicon, 1600, which are connected with the Works of Shakespeare. Small quarto, 1865. *Out of Print.*

17. Extracts taken from the Vestry-book of the Church of the Holy Trinity at Stratford-on-Avon, containing Entries illustrative of the History of that Church, with several Notices of the Shakespeare Family. Small quarto, 1865. *Out of Print.*

18. A Nominal Index to J. O. Halliwell's Descriptive Calendar of the Ancient Records of Stratford-on-Avon. Octavo, 1865. *Out of Print.*

19. A Levy made in July, 1697, for the Relief of the Poor at Stratford-on-Avon ; the earliest one yet discovered. Now first Printed from the original MS. Quarto, 1865. *Out of Print.*

20. Collectanea respecting the Birth-Place of Shakespeare at

E

Stratford-on-Avon, copied from the MS. Collections of the late R. B. Wheler. With a few Additions. Quarto, 1865. *Out of Print.*

21. Some Account of Robert Chester's Loves Martyr, or Rosalin's Complaint, a very rare volume published in the year 1601, including a remarkable Poem by Shakespeare. With facsimiles by E. W. Ashbee. Small quarto, 1865. *Out of Print.*

22. A Copy of a Letter of News written to Sir Dudley Carleton at the Hague in May, 1619, containing a curious Account of the Performance of the Drama of Pericles at the English Court. Square 12mo. 1865. *Out of Print.*

23. Original Memoirs and Historical Accounts of the Families of Shakespeare and Hart, deduced from an early period, and continued down to this present year 1790. By John Jordan of Stratford-on-Avon. Quarto, 1865. *Out of Print.*

24. Indentures respecting the Cage, a House in High Street, Stratford-on-Avon, inhabited by Thomas Quiney, son-in-law to Shakespeare, 1616-1633. Square 12mo. 1865. *Out of Print.*

25.* Shaksperian Parallelisms chiefly illustrative of the Tempest and A Midsummer Night's Dream, collected from Sydney's Arcadia. Square 12mo. 1865.

26.* Some Account of the Popular Belief in Animated Horse-hairs, alluded to by Shakespeare in the Play of Antony and Cleopatra. Square 12mo. 1866.

27.* The Tale of Tereus and Progne referred to several Times by Shakespeare. Square 12mo. 1866.

28.* Papers respecting Disputes which arose from Incidents at the Death-bed of Richard Tarlton the Actor in the year 1588. Square 12mo. 1866.

29.* The Last Will and Testament of John Davenant, vintner, of the Crown Tavern, Oxford, the house at which Shakespeare lodged in some of his Journeys between Stratford-on-Avon and London. Square 12mo. 1866.

30.* The Booke of Merry Riddles, together with proper Questions and witty Proverbs, to make pleasant Pastime. Square 12mo. 1866.

31.* Acolastus his Afterwritte, a Poem by S. Nicholson,

1600, containing singular Plagiarisms from Shakespeare. Quarto, 1866.

32.* Extracts from the Accounts of the Chamberlains of the Borough of Stratford-on-Avon, from the year 1585 to 1608. Selected and edited from the original Manuscripts. Small Quarto, 1866.

33.* The Accounts of the Chamberlains of the Borough of Stratford-on-Avon, from the year 1590 to the year 1597; now first edited from the original Manuscript. Small quarto, 1866.

34.* A Discovery that Shakespeare wrote one or more Ballads or Poems on the Spanish Armada. Small quarto, 1866.

35.* Abstracts and Copies of Indentures respecting Estates in Henley Street, Stratford-on-Avon, which illustrate the Topography and History of the Birthplace of Shakespeare. Quarto, 1866.

ENTIRE FACSIMILES IN SMALL QUARTO

VOLUMES,

OF ALL THE EDITIONS OF

THE PLAYS OF SHAKESPEARE,

WHICH WERE PRINTED BEFORE THE

FIRST FOLIO OF 1623;

AND OF THOSE EDITIONS OF THE POEMS WHICH

WERE PRINTED IN QUARTO.

SHAKESPEARE FACSIMILES.

NO library does, and probably no library ever will, contain a perfect set of the early separate editions of Shakespeare's Plays. Even the British Museum and Bodleian libraries together fail to supply the student with some of the most important and valuable; and feeling the inestimable importance to the student of all these pieces, I have long desired to preserve such a series to the use of critics.

No expense will be spared in rendering every volume of undoubted accuracy and authenticity. At first sight, it might appear that nothing was easier than to secure this; but a large proportion of the early editions now existing have been more or less "made up" with facsimile, or with, what is far more dangerous, other copies, thus involving a risk of part of a copy being of another edition, the signatures and catch-words of several editions corresponding.

Nothing but the greatest care, and long practice and experience, will prevent the risk of errors arising from such circumstances. I shall exercise the greatest vigilance in endeavouring to make the series *absolutely reliable as a permanent reference and authority*, and, if I am encouraged to complete it, I think I may venture to say (as the names of the artists only will appear, I being the director, not the worker), that it will form one of the most important contributions to English literature ever executed.

The facsimiles are executed on lithographic plates, each *page* being a *separate* plate on fine paper : a plan far more convenient to the student for collation and comparison than an attempted imitation of the old quarto pamphlet, which latter may properly be objected to as one likely to deceive posterity.

The impression will be most strictly limited to *thirty-one* copies *only*, each copy being numbered by myself, and attested further *by both artist and binder*.

The greatest pains will be taken to render these thirty-one copies fine perfect ones, and to adhere most strictly to the limit. The lithographers have the strictest injunctions to carry out this intention. The plan will be as follows. They will strike off fifty copies, all on fine paper, out of which the binders will select thirty-one of the best and clearest impressions for binding, after which the remaining nineteen copies will be destroyed, *such destruction being attested in each copy, and every copy being numbered in writing.*

The whole of these facsimiles are being executed by Mr. Ashhee, whose reputation as a lithographic artist is a guarantee for their excellence and accuracy.

Now Ready.

1. The History of Henrie the Fourth, with the Battell at Shrewsburie betweene the King and Lord Henry Percy, surnamed Henry Hotspur of the North, with the humorous conceits of Sir Iohn Falstaffe. Quarto, 1599. *Out of print separately.*

2. The Tragedie of King Richard the Second, as it hath beene publikely acted by the Right Honourable the Lorde Chamberlaine his seruants. Quarto, 1597. *Out of print separately.*

3. The Late and much admired Play called Pericles Prince of Tyre, with the true relation of the whole Historie, adventures and fortunes of the said Prince, as also the accidents, &c. in the Birth and Life of his daughter Mariana. By William Shakespeare. Quarto, 1609. *Out of print separately.*

4. The Tragedy of King Richard the Third, as it hath beene lately Acted by the Right Honourable the Lord Chamberlaine his seruants. Quarto, 1597. *Out of print separately.*

F

5. The Famous Historie of Troylus and Cresseid. Excellently expressing the beginning of their loves, with the conceited wooing of Pandarus Prince of Licia. Written by William Shakespeare. Quarto, 1609. *Out of print separately.*

6. A Midsommer Nights Dreame. As it hath beene sundry times publikely acted by the Right Honourable the Lord Chamberlaine his Servants. Written by William Shakespeare. Quarto. Imprinted at London for Thomas Fisher, 1600. *Out of print separately.*

7. The Tragœdy of Othello, the Moore of Venice. As it hath beene diverse times acted at the Globe and at the Black-Friers by his Maiesties Servants. Written by William Shakespeare. Quarto, 1622. *Out oy print separately.*

8. The Tragedie of King Richard the Third, conteining his treacherous Plots against his brother Clarence, &c, with the whole course of his detested life, and most deserved Death. Newly augmented. By William Shake-speare. Quarto, 1605. *Out oy print separately.*

9. Much Ado about Nothing, as it hath been sundrie Times publikely acted by the Right Honourable the Lord Chamberlaine his Servants. Written by William Shakespeare. Quarto, 1600. *Out of print separately.*

10. The most excellent and lamentable Tragedie of Romeo and Juliet, newly corrected, augmented and amended, As it hath bene sundry Times publiquely acted by the Right Honourable the Lord Chamberlaine his Servants. Quarto, 1599.

11. The Tragedie of King Richard the Third, conteining his treacherous Plots against his brother Clarence, the pittifull murther of his innocent Nephewes, &c. Newly augmented by William Shakespeare. Quarto, 1602. *Out of print separately.*

12. The Excellent History of the Merchant of Venice, with the extreme Cruelty of Shylocke the Jew towards the saide Merchant in cutting a just Pound of his Flesh, and the obtaining of Portia by the choyse of three Caskets. Written by W. Shakespeare. Printed by J. Roberts. Quarto, 1600. *Out of print separately.*

13. A Midsummer Night's Dreame, as it hath beene sundry Times publikely acted by the Right Honourable the Lord Chamberlaine his Servants. Written by William Shakespeare. Printed by James Roberts. Quarto, 1600.

14. The most lamentable Romaine Tragedie of Titus Andronicus, as it hath sundry Times beene playde by the Right Honourable the Earle of Pembroke, the Earle of Darbie, the

Earle of Sussex, and the Lord Chamberlaine, theyr Seruants. Quarto, 1600.

15. A Most Pleasant and excellent conceited Comedy of Sir John Falstaffe and the Merry Wives of Windsor, with the swaggering vaine of Ancient Pistoll and Corporal Nym. Written by W. Shakespeare. Quarto, 1619.

16. Lucrece. Quarto, 1594.

17. The Tragicall Historie of Hamlet, Prince of Denmarke. By William Shake-speare. As it hath beene diverse Times acted by his Highnesse Servants in the Cittie of London, as also in the two Universities of Cambridge and Oxford, and elsewhere. Quarto, 1603.

18. The Second Part of Henrie the Fourth, continuing to his Death, and Coronation of Henrie the Fift. With the Humours of Sir John Falstaffe and Swaggering Pistoll. As it hath been sundrie times publikely acted by the Right Honourable the Lord Chamberlaine his Servants. Written by William Shakespeare. Quarto, 1600.

19. The Second Part of Henrie the Fourth, continuing to his

Death, and Coronation of Henrie the Fift. Quarto, 1600. This is the second edition, with the same title as the preceding, but containing four more pages.

20. A Most Pleasaunt and excellent conceited Comedie of Syr John Falstaffe and the Merrie Wives of Windsor. Enter-mixed with sundrie variable and pleasing Humors of Syr Hugh the Welch Knight, Justice Shallow, and his wise cousin M. Slender. With the swaggering vaine of Auncient Pistoll and Corporal Nym. By William Shakespeare. As it hath bene divers times Acted by the Right Honorable my Lord Chamberlaines Servants, both before her Majestie and else-where. Quarto, 1602.

21. Venus and Adonis. Quarto, 1593.

A List of the Editions to be Facsimiled, completing the Series.

22. The Tragedie of King Richard the Second, with new Additions of the Parliament Sceane, and the Deposing of King Richard. Quarto, 1608.

23. The Most Excellent Historie of the Merchant of Venice, with the extreame Crueltie of Shylocke the Jewe towards the

sayd Merchant, &c. London, Printed by I. R. for Thomas Heyes, 1600.

24. The Historie of Henry the Fourth, With the Battell at Shrewseburie. Quarto, 1622.

25. The Cronicle History of Henry the Fift, with his Battell fought at Agincourt in France. Quarto, 1600.

26. M. William Shake-speare, His True Chronicle History of the Life and Death of King Lear. The edition with no place of sale named in the imprint. Quarto, 1608.

27. The Tragedie of King Richard the Third, containing his Treacherous Plots against his Brother Clarence. Quarto, 1612.

28. The Late and much admired Play called Pericles, Prince of Tyre. Quarto, 1619.

29. The Most Excellent and Lamentable Tragedie of Romeo and Juliet, as it hath beene sundrie Times publikely Acted. London, Printed for John Smethwicke. Quarto, n. d.

30. The Tragicall Historie of Hamlet, Prince of Denmarke. By William Shakespeare. Newly imprinted and enlarged to the true and perfect Coppie. Quarto, 1604.

31. The History of Henry the Fourth, with the Battell at Shrewseburie. Quarto, 1608.

32.* The Chronicle History of Henry the Fift, with his Battell fought at Agincourt in France. Quarto, 1602.

33. The most excellent and Lamentable Tragedie of Romeo and Juliet, as it hath beene sundrie Times publiquely acted by the Kings Majesties Servants at the Globe. Quarto, 1609.

34. The Tragedy of Hamlet, Prince of Denmarke, newly imprinted and inlarged according to the true and perfect copy lastly printed. Quarto. Printed by W. S. for John Smethwicke, n. d.

35. The Tragedie of King Richard the Second, as it hath been publikely acted by the Right Honourable the Lord Chamberlaine his Servants. Quarto, 1608.

36.* The Historie of Henrie the Fourth, with the Battell at Shrewsburie betweene the King and Lord Henry Percy, surnamed Henry Hotspur of the North. Quarto, 1604.

37. The Chronicle History of Henry the Fift, with his Battell fought at Agincourt in France. Quarto, 1608.

38. The Tragedie of King Richard the Third, contayning his treacherous Plots against his brother Clarence. Quarto, 1622.

39. The most lamentable Tragedie of Titus Andronicus. As it hath sundry times beene plaide by the Kings Majesties Servants. Quarto, 1611.

40. The History of Henrie the Fourth, with the Battell at Shrewseburie. Quarto, 1613.

41. The Late and much admired Play called Pericles Prince of Tyre. Quarto, 1611.

42. The Tragedy of Hamlet, Prince of Denmarke, newly imprinted and enlarged to almost as much againe as it was. Quarto, 1611.

43. The Tragedie of King Richard the Third, conteining his treacherous Plots against his brother Clarence. Quarto, 1598.

44. An Excellent Conceited Tragedie of Romeo and Juliet, as it hath been often with great applause plaid publiquely. Quarto, 1597.

45. The Tragicall Historie of Hamlet, Prince of Denmarke.

By William Shakespeare. Newly imprinted and enlarged to almost as much againe as it was. Quarto, 1605.

46. Venus and Adonis. Quarto, 1594.

47. Shakespeare's Sonnets, never before Imprinted. At London, to be solde by John Wright dwelling at Christ Church Gate. Quarto, 1609.

48. The Tragedie of King Richard the Second, with new Additions of the Parliament Sceane, and the deposing of King Richard. Quarto, 1615.

49. A Pleasant Conceited Comedie called Loves Labors Lost. Quarto, 1598.

50. The Tragedie of King Richard the Second, as it hath beene publiquely acted by the Right Honourable the Lord Chamberlaine his Servants. Quarto, 1598.

51. The History of Henrie the Fourth, with the Battell at Shrewsburie betwene the King and Lord Henry Percy, surnamed Henrie Hotspur of the North. Quarto, 1598.

52. M. William Shak-speare, his True Chronicle Historie of

G

the Life and Death of King Lear and his Three Daughters. The London edition, with the place of sale in the imprint. Quarto, 1608.

53. Shakespeare's Sonnets. At London, by G. Eld for T. T. and are to be solde by William Aspley. Quarto, 1609.

54. The Historie of Troylus and Cresseida, as it was acted by the Kings Majesties Servants at the Globe. Quarto, 1609. The second edition of the previous one bearing the same date.

These fifty-four volumes comprise every one of Shakespeare's plays issued before the publication of the first folio in 1623, as well as all the early editions of the poems which appeared in a quarto form. The later editions of the poems in duodecimo are of no critical value and would not range uniformly with this series; to say nothing of the cost of including them, which would entail an additional expense of £63 upon every subscriber without a corresponding advantage.

Subscribers to the Entire Series.

The subscription of those who subscribed to the entire series before the 1st of August, 1866, is five guineas each volume for fifty volumes, four volumes being presented. To any one now subscribing to the series, the whole of the fifty-four volumes will be charged at the same rate, viz. five guineas per volume.

Subscribers to Separate Volumes.

Those numbers not marked as " out of print separately" can at present be subscribed for at five guineas per volume.

Preparing for the Press, by Subscription, and for Subscribers

only, in Folio Volumes, profusely illustrated by

Engravings on Wood,

ILLUSTRATIONS OF THE LIFE AND WRITINGS OF

WILLIAM SHAKESPEARE,

BY J. O. HALLIWELL, ESQ. F. R. S.

ILLUSTRATIONS, Etc.

I T is proposed in a series of folio volumes to accumulate a collection of materials illustrative of the details of Shakespeare's Life and Works, in which, amongst other matters, the Stratford-on-Avon, the London, and the England of the Poet's day will be attempted to be interpreted by the aid of contemporary documents and books, and by an elaborate system of truthful artistic illustration.

I wish at the same time to produce a work which shall be creditable as a specimen of English typography. It is curious that the art of printing should have reached to perfection soon after its introduction, and that no modern books equal some of the old ones in their execution. If encouraged, I will spare neither pains nor expense in an attempt to emulate the finest examples of the ancient presses.

The public will, I hope, enable me to do this. It is of no use at all commencing the work, unless these ideas can be carried out with ample means and on a liberal scale of expenditure. I can fortunately afford to work at these grateful studies without the prospect of remuneration, but not to incur the loss of the many thousand pounds an inadequate subscription list would here entail ; and works of this kind, unless one is prepared to sustain an excessive pecuniary loss, can only be printed by subscription.

My materials will be purposely arranged in a disconnected form. Thus, an account of Anne Hathaway's Cottage may be followed by notes on Hamlet, and so on ; the object of this being that the work could be relinquished at any time without being rendered imperfect. A second title, not marked as for a series, will be furnished with the first volume, so that whether ten volumes are issued, or only one, the work will yet be a complete one in itself.

The following Conditions of Subscription have been studiously framed in the interests of the subscribers. The destruction of the woodblocks will, I am aware, be considered by some as a barbarous act, but it is the only step I know of which effectually precludes their being used hereafter in a cheaper work.

CONDITIONS OF SUBSCRIPTION.

1. The subscription to each volume shall be four guineas, and no more than one subscription volume shall be issued in a year.

2. The subscription list on the above terms shall finally close on the   day of

₊ This date will be determined upon when the subscription list is further advanced.

3. After the subscription list is closed on the day just before mentioned, no one shall be received as a subscriber on the original terms; but the Editor shall be at liberty to print a number of surplus copies beyond those subscribed for, *not exceeding eighty*, but he shall not part with a single one of such surplus copies without receiving a premium in addition to the original subscription, of *at least* twenty guineas.

4. Not a single perfect copy shall be made up out of the waste, which shall be exclusively devoted to the completion of copies that may be soiled or damaged, or by any cause, rendered imperfect.

5. The names and addresses of all the subscribers shall be printed in each volume in the order in which their names are received.

6. Liberty is reserved to remove the name of any subscriber

H

who is two years in arrear of payment of his subscription.

7. Subscribers resident in the United States, in the Colonies, or in foreign countries, shall make arrangements which will relieve the Editor of trouble in regard to the subscriptions, and of expense or risk in the delivery of the work.

8. Liberty is reserved to make special subscription arrangements with libraries of a strictly permanent character.

9. All the woodblocks used in this work shall be destroyed as the work proceeds.

10. These rules or conditions of subscription shall not be subject to any alteration.

The Life of Shakespeare.

Within the last few years I have enjoyed unrivalled facilities for investigating this subject, and have accumulated a large quantity of new materials. The voluminous ancient records of Stratford-on-Avon have been so freely accessible to me that I have read every line of the many thousand documents there preserved, not even excluding jury-lists. The Corporation of that town have kindly aided my researches to the fullest extent of their power, even to the opening of attics that had been closed for centuries, and to searches between the rafters of their ancient Council-house. In addition to these opportunities, the masses of papers accumulated in the old established legal offices at Stratford have been carefully explored, the whole yielding an assemblage of useful materials far larger than I heretofore thought could have been preserved.

THE WOODCUT ILLUSTRATIONS.

All the illustrations to this work will be engraved on wood, even the facsimiles of old print and writing, which, by a new though expensive * process, can be so engraved with perfect accuracy, and with an effect superior, I think, to that produced by any other method. The illustrations will consist of views of churches, old houses, scenery, portraits, articles of domestic use, costume, music, plans, facsimiles, plants, birds, flowers, animals,

---

* I find that the facsimile thus executed of a *single* document has cost me no less than *thirty-eight pounds,* a fact I mention to suggest to the readers of this prospectus how large a support at the low rate of sub-scription here indicated must be given, with any chance of my expenses being met.

&c; in short, of everything, especially what is old English, that can in any degree illustrate the text of Shakespeare, or realise to us any glimpses of his life in London or in the country. The old rural life in Warwickshire will be attempted to be illustrated both by the aid of pencil and of any the minutest facts that can throw light upon it, even if they be of the humble class—

> Which Wisdom may disdain to hear,
> And Learning may not understand.

SHAKESPEARIAN COMMENTARY.

In estimating the value of Shakespearian criticism, the distinction between its relative and comparative importance is too often lost sight of. Relatively to the text, it is the most important study in English literature; viewed comparatively with that text, it sinks into insignificance. I would not surrender the little Induction to the Taming of the Shrew in exchange for all the results, present and future, of all Shakespearian criticism. On the other hand, the true restoration of a single line in Shakespeare is well worth the best volume of any other English writer.

The true secret of the dislike in some quarters to Shakespeare Commentary is, I believe, to be found in the baseless fancy that the critics seek an alliance in the matter of fame with his imperishable glory. As well might one accuse the commentators on the Bible of a wish to be thought inspired. Shakespeare, like the Bible, is the easiest book to understand in one sense— the most difficult in another. A little patient study of the subject will convince any one that the Works of Shakespeare require and deserve, for their complete interpretation, a larger amount of commentary than do those of any other English writer.

Illustrations of the Biography.

The artistic illustration of Shakespearian objects of interest in Warwickshire is as yet in its infancy, a remark which applies not merely to obscure points of interest, but to those memorials the delineations of which may have been naturally thought to be exhausted. For example, the Birth-Place of the Poet has been the subject of a thousand engravings, but the same ground has been traversed in all. We have the general exterior, the shop, the kitchen, and the birth-room over and over again ; but no details of the various other portions of the building, no systematic attempt to trace the history of the edifice by the reproduction of old sketches ; in short, no original investigation. Thus, the ancient cellar of the Birth-Place, the only room in the house which retains its precise original features, and which was no doubt a familiar spot to the boy-Poet, has hitherto entirely escaped observation.

The reason of this apparent negligence* arises from the circumstance of no artist having yet resided sufficiently long for the purpose at Stratford-on-Avon. A hasty visit of a few weeks does not suffice. Mr. J. T. Blight and myself have spent summer after summer in the locality, exploring every nook and corner in our power, and yet in Chapel Street, a spot of all others we had carefully investigated, the accidental opening of a door (generally closed) revealed at the last moment one of the choicest genuine fragments of Shakespeare's Stratford. Mr. Blight has made for this work the almost incredible number of *six hundred and thirty-two* original sketches of old houses, scenery, and details of archæological remains in the locality of Stratford and its neighbourhood *alone*.

The noble parish-church of Stratford-on-Avon is so intimately associated with the history of Shakespeare, it is proposed to engrave in detail every portion of the sacred edifice.

In addition to Mr. Blight's original sketches, numerous photographs, and I believe a complete series of all engravings of the slightest value, I have obtained every old drawing bearing on the subject that could be secured, so that the collection of artistic objects accumulated for use in this work is unrivalled in extent

---

* I do not of course exclude myself from whatever of censure may be here implied. When, in 1853, I had printed the Life of Shakespeare, in the first volume of my folio edition, I was goose enough to fancy that I had then exhausted the subject.

and interest, one which could not now be formed by any amount of expenditure.

The value of the sketches, both the old and the modern ones, is immensely enhanced by the alterations so rapidly progressing in Stratford and the neighbourhood. Even during the last year or two, several objects of interest sketched by Mr. Blight have either disappeared, or lost their ancient characteristic features. One cannot mention without emotions of deep regret what was until lately the most charming of the environs of Stratford, the mill-bridge and the weir-brake, a locality traditionally associated with Shakespeare, and one with which he must have been familiar. All the picturesque character of this spot is now for ever ruined by the advent of one of those noxious railways which are destroying the scenery of England, obliterating its rural character, substituting the hideous noise of a screaming whistle for the harmony of birds, and gradually even exiling quiet thoughts. We are passing now into a new order of things, and I have been only just in time to preserve a glimpse of that England which Shakespeare loved.

LIST OF SUBSCRIBERS TO JANUARY 1ST, 1867.

His Royal Highness the Prince of Wales, K.G.

1. The Right Hon. Lord Houghton.
2. W. O. Hunt, Clerk of the Peace for Warwickshire, Stratford-on-Avon.
3. John Staunton, Esq. Longbridge House, near Warwick.
4. William Powell Hunt, Esq. Solicitor, Ipswich.
5. Sterling Westhorp, Esq. Ipswich.
6. John Blake Jell, Esq. Sydenham, Kent.
7. The Right Hon. the Earl of Warwick.
8. Henry Huth, Esq. 30, Princes Gate, London.
9. F. W. Cosens, Esq. Clapham Park, London.
10. Frederick Ouvry, Esq. F.S.A. 12, Queen Anne Street, Cavendish Square.
11. Thomas Combs, Esq. Dorchester.
12. Robert McConnell, Esq. Merchant, Liverpool.
13. Benjamin Godfrey Windus, Esq. Tottenham Green, Middlesex.
14. Charles Walton, Esq. the Manor House, East Acton.
15. E. W. Ashbee, Esq. 17, Mornington Crescent.
16. Travers B. Wire, Esq. Crooms Hill, Blackheath.
17. William James Clement, Esq. M.P. the Council House, Shrewsbury.

18. His Grace the Duke of Buccleuch and Queensberry, K.G.

19. Frederick Haines, Esq. F.S.A. Maida Hill.

20. The Rev. Thomas Halliwell, M.A. Brighton.

21. Charles Winn, Esq. Nostel Priory, Wakefield.

22. The Society of Antiquaries of London, Somerset House.

23. Thomas Turpin, Esq. Brighton.

24. The Right Hon. Lord Farnham, K.P.

25. The Bodleian Library, Oxford.

26. William Harrison, Esq. F.S.A. Galligreaves Hall, Blackburn.

27. James Pilkington, Esq. Park Place House, Blackburn.

28. Samuel Timmins, Esq. Birmingham.

29. William Horsfall, Esq. Dunham Massey, Cheshire.

30. Bell Fletcher, M.D. Birmingham.

31. William Euing, Esq. Glasgow.

32. The Liverpool Free Public Library.

33. John Camden Hotten, Esq. 74, Piccadilly.

34. Henry Stevens, Esq. G.M.B., F.S.A.

35. Captain Henry Ward, 45, Gloucester Street, S.W.

36. A. M'Laren Brown, Esq. 267, Camden Road.

37. George C. E. Bacon, Esq. Ipswich.

38. Charles Henry Elt, Esq. 1, Noel Street, Islington.

39. Hastings Elwin, Esq. Horstead House, near Norwich.

40. John Addis, Esq. jun. Rustington, Sussex.

41. Fred. Blackman, Esq. Surgeon, 4, York Road.

42. The Rev. J. H. Ellis, M.A. King's Road, Clapham Park.

43. Alexander Ireland, Esq. Manchester.

44. J. Wyllie Guild, Esq. Park Circus, Glasgow.

45. John Alfred Langford, Esq. Birmingham.

46. H. M. Beck, Esq. Junymount, Belfast.

47. The London Institution, Finsbury Circus.

48. Henry Parnall, Esq. Bishopsgate Street.

49. Thomas Falconer, Esq. Usk.

50. Walter J. Sackett, Esq. Birmingham.

51. G. W. Whistler, Esq. Frankfort-on-Maine.

52. Alexander Smollett, Esq. of Bonhill, N.B.

53. The Library of the Corporation of London.

54. Paul Walmsley, Esq. Manchester.

55. W. H. Brown, Esq. Solicitor, Chester.

56. William Leaf, Esq. Park Hill, Streatham.

57. His Grace the Duke of Devonshire, K.G.

58. John E. Howe, Esq. Manchester.

59. John Wilkinson, Esq. F.S.A.

60. Thomas Hewitt, Esq. A.M. Cork.

61. J. Watts Russell, Esq. D.C.L., F.R.S.

62. S. Whitney Phœnix, Esq. New York.

63. Archibald Orr Ewing, Esq. Ballikinsain, Glasgow.

64. The Rev. O. T. Dobbin, LL.D. Meath.

65. The South Kensington Museum, Art Library.

66. The South Kensington Museum, Educational Library.

67. George W. Nichols, Esq. Almond Tree House, Rother-
hithe.

68. The Rev. Robert Scarr Redfern, M.A. Vicar of Acton,
Nautwich, Cheshire.

69. G. Crowther, Esq. Carlisle.

70. H. R. Forrest, Esq. Grindlow House, Longsight, Manchester.

71. J. Russell Smith, Esq. 36, Soho Square.

72. H. T. Hall, Esq. Cambridge.

73. John Haes, Esq. Clapham Rise.

74. Charles Rothwell, Esq. Bolton.

75. The Public Library, Penzance.

76. I. de Witte van Citters, the Hague.

77. Alexander Young, Esq. Glasgow.

78. The Rev. G. A. Pauton, Glasgow.

79 to 83. Messrs. Sampson Low, Son and Marston, Milton
House, Ludgate Hill.

84. Charles Holte Bracebridge, Esq. Atherstone Hall.

85. The Chetham Library, Manchester.

86. The Rev. E. L. Barnwell, M.A. Bath.

87. Robert Lang, Esq. Gratwicke Hall, Barrow-Gurney, near
Bristol.

88. William Skeffington, Esq. 163, Piccadilly.

89. Captain H. St. John Mildmay.

90, 91. Messrs. Lockwood and Co. No. 7, Stationers' Hall Court.

92. Mrs. Henry Drummond, Hunton, Staplehurst.

93. E. T. Carson, Esq. Cincinuati, U.S.

94. T. Thorneycroft Kesteven, Esq. Hamstead House, near Birmingham.

95.· W. A. Harris, Esq. Balliol College, Oxford.

In answer to numerous enquiries, any Subscriber may withdraw within two months after the production of any volume. Thus the utmost sum a person now subscribing need be liable for will be four guineas; but if he does not withdraw within two months after the publication of the first volume, he will be liable to another subscription of four guineas; if he does not withdraw within two months after the publication of the second volume, he will be liable to a third subscription of four guineas; and so on. It is absolutely necessary that early notice should be given of withdrawal, otherwise I shall be at a loss to know what sum will be available for the production of the next volume; but the present arrangement will dispose of that question of liability which, I find, deters many from subscribing.

The nature of the work must not be misunderstood. It will not be a mere collection of shreds and patches, but a series of Shakespearian treatises, compiled with great labour, dispersedly arranged, so that, should the work arrive at an early termination, it will still be a perfect book in the sense in which book-buyers use that expression. And so large a support will be required to meet the expenses, perhaps I may be excused indulging the hope that its character of a quaint picture-book (including much which will be illustrative of ancient art) will recommend it to the favour of many who may take no special interest in abstruse researches, and even obtain for it a place on the drawing-room table.

NOTE.

Should anyone into whose hands this pamphlet may fall know of the existence of copies of early editions of Shakespeare in private hands, especially any for sale, they would confer the greatest favour by communicating with me at No. 6, St. Mary's Place, West Brompton, near London.

I am very anxious to obtain an imperfect copy of Love's Labour's Lost, 1598, which was sold by auction at Messrs. Sotheby's on November 22nd, 1826, for two pounds six shillings. It was bought by the late Mr. Thorpe, but all endeavours to trace it further have failed. Now if this copy has the first three leaves of text in fine condition, I shall be happy to give one hundred guineas for it, or the same sum for any other copy having those leaves. Care must be taken to ascertain that the leaves are really original, Malone having privately made a fac-simile reprint.

J. O. H.

www.ingramcontent.com/pod-product-compliance
Lightning Source LLC
Chambersburg PA
CBHW021512090426
42739CB00007B/573